ETHICS AND

MW01005333

R.C. SPROUL
ETHICS AND
THE CHRISTIAN

Tyndale House
Publishers, Inc.
Wheaton, Illinois

Third printing, August 1986

Library of Congress Catalog Card Number 83-50059
ISBN 0-8423-0775-3, paper
Copyright © 1983 R.C. Sproul
Printed in the United States of America

CONTENTS

INTRODUCTION

Almost every major book on ethics published today devotes its first chapter to an analysis of the chaotic situation that our culture faces in the area of ethics. Not only is there a recognition of this chaos, but even among secular thinkers and ethicists, there is a sense of urgency calling for some basic agreement for ethical behavior to be reached because "man's margin of error" becomes increasingly diminished as time passes. The survival of mankind is at stake. The "prophets of doom" in the area of international affairs maintain that man's destructive capability increased by the same ratio between 1945 and 1960 as it did from the Stone Age, the age of the primitive bow and arrow, to the dropping of the bomb on Hiroshima. This stark reality, coupled with the pressing needs of social justice, the specter of international terrorism, and the sense of aimlessness in personal and social ethics, demands a resolution. One technical volume, Hill's *Contemporary Ethical Theories,* canvasses more than eighty divergent theories of ethics competing for acceptance in our modern world. This proliferation of options generates confusion and, for many, a sense of despair about reaching a cultural consensus that would stabilize the shifting sands of pluralism.

The study of ethics is a complex matter. We must proceed with a spirit of soberness and thoroughness, lest we satisfy ourselves with a simplistic approach to questions of great importance. Ethics can never be understood divorced and isolated from other intellectual dimensions of life. No field is immune from ethical judgments. In politics, in psychology, in medicine, in all disciplines, ethical decisions are made regularly. The legislative action, the economic policy, the school board's curriculum, the psychiatrist's advice—all involve ethical considerations. Every vote cast in the ballot box marks an ethical decision.

ONE
ETHICS AND MORALS

In present word usage the term "ethics" is often used interchangeably with the word "morals" or "morality." That the two have become virtual synonyms is a sign of the confusion which permeates the modern ethical scene. Historically, the two words had quite distinctive meanings. Ethics comes from the Greek *ethos,* which derived from the root word meaning "stall," a place for horses. It conveyed the sense of a dwelling place, a place of stability and permanence. On the other hand, morality comes from the word "mores" which describes the behavioral patterns of a given society.

Ethics is a normative science, searching for the principal foundations that prescribe obligations or "oughtness." It is concerned primarily with the imperative and with the philosophical premises upon which imperatives are based. Morality is a descriptive science, concerned with "isness" and the indicative. Morals describe what people do; ethics define what people ought to do. The difference between them is between the normal and the normative.

Ethics	Morals
1. normative	1. descriptive
2. imperative	2. indicative
3. oughtness	3. isness
4. absolute	4. relative

When morality is identified with ethics, the normal becomes the normative and the imperative is swallowed by the status quo. This creates a kind of "statistical morality." In this schema the good is determined by the normal and the normal is determined by the statistical average. The "norm" is discovered by an analysis of the normal, or by counting noses. Conformity to that norm then becomes the ethical obligation. It works like this:

Step #1. We compile an analysis of statistical behavior patterns such as those integral to the Kinsey Report and the Chapman Report. If we discover that a majority of people are in fact participating in premarital sexual intercourse, then we declare such activity "normal."

Step #2. We move quickly from the normal to a description of what is authentically "human." Humanness is defined by what human beings do. Hence, if the normal human being engages in premarital sexual intercourse, we conclude that such activity is normal and therefore "good."

Step #3. The third step is to declare patterns which deviate from the normal to be *abnormal, inhuman,* and *inauthentic.* In this schema chastity becomes a form of deviate sexual behavior and the stigma is placed on the virgin rather than the non-virgin.

Statistical morality operates on the following syllogism:

Premise A—the normal is determined by statistics;
Premise B—the normal is human and good;
        —the abnormal is inhuman and bad.

In this humanistic approach to ethics the highest good (*summum bonum*) is defined by that activity which is most authentically human. This method achieves great popularity when applied to some issues but breaks down when applied to others. If we do a statistical analysis of the experience of cheating among students or lying among the general public, we discover that a majority of students have at some time practiced cheating and that all men have sometimes practiced lying. If the canons of statistical morality apply, the only verdict we can render is that cheating is an authentically human good and that lying is a *bona fide* virtue.

Obviously there must be a relationship between our ethical theories and our moral behavior. In a real sense our beliefs dictate our behavior. A theory underlies our every moral action. We may not be able to articulate that theory or even be immediately conscious of it, but nothing manifests our value systems more sharply than our actions.

The Christian ethic is based on an antithesis between what is and what ought to be. We view the world as fallen; an analysis of fallen human be-

11

havior describes what is normal to the abnormal situation of human corruption. God calls us out of the indicative by His imperative. Ours is a call to nonconformity—to a transforming ethic that shatters the status quo.

Even within relativistic claims, a serious inconsistency emerges. The decade of the sixties brought a moral revolution to our culture, spearheaded by the protests of the youth. Two slogans were repeated, broadcast side by side during this movement. The tension was captured by these twin slogans: "Tell it like it is" and "Do your own thing."

The cry for personal freedom was encapsulated in the "inalienable right" to do one's own thing. This was a demand for subjective freedom of self-expression. When the guns were turned on the older generation, however, a curious and glaring inconsistency was heard: "Tell it like it is." This slogan implies an objective basis for truth and virtue. The adult generation was not "allowed" to do their own thing if doing their own thing deviated from objective norms of truth. The flower children demanded the right to have their ethical cake and eat it too.

I was once maneuvered into an unenviable counseling situation by a distraught Christian mother, performing the role of a modern day Monica anguishing over the wayward behavior of her non-believing and rebellious son. The lad had retreated from his mother's constant religious and moral directives by moving out of the family home and into his own apartment. He promptly decorated his apartment with walls painted black and strobe lights flashing, then adorned the room with accoutrements designed for the liberal indulgence of hashish and other exotic drugs. His was a bacchanalian "pad" into which he promptly invited a willing co-ed to join him in luxurious cohabitation. All of this was to his mother's unmitigated horror. I agreed to talk with the young man only after explaining to the mother that such an encounter would probably engender further hostility. I would be viewed as the mother's "hired gun." The youth also agreed to the meeting obviously only to escape further verbal harassment from his mother.

When the young man appeared at my office, he was overtly hostile and obviously wanted to get the meeting over with as quickly as possible. I began the interview bluntly by asking directly, "Who are you mad at?"

Without hesitation he growled, "My mother."

"Why?" I inquired.

"Because all she does is hassle me. She keeps trying to shove religion down my throat."

I went on to inquire what alternative value system he had embraced in place of his mother's ethical system. He replied, "I believe everyone ought to be free to do his own thing."

I then asked, "Does that include your mother?" He was startled by the question and not immediately aware of what I was driving at. I explained to him that if he embraced a Christian ethic he could readily enlist me as an ally in his cause. His mother had been harsh, provoking her son to wrath and being insensitive to questions and feelings, issues which are indeed circumscribed by the biblical ethic. I explained that at several crucial points his mother had violated Christian ethics. However, I pointed out that on the boy's ethical terms he had no legitimate gripe. "Maybe your mother's 'thing' is to harass children by shoving religion down their throats. How can you possibly object to that?" It became clear that the boy wanted everybody (especially himself) to have the right to do his or her "own thing" except when or unless the other person's "thing" impinged on *his* "thing."

It is commonplace to hear the lament that some Christians, notably conservatives, are so rigidly bound by moralistic guidelines that everything becomes for them a matter of "black and white" with no room left for "gray" areas. Those who persist in fleeing from the gray, seeking refuge in the sharply defined areas of white and black, suffer from the epitaph "brittle" or "dogmatic." But the Christian must seek for righteousness and never be satisfied with living in the smog of perpetual grayness. He wants to know where the right way is located, where the path of righteousness lies.

There is a right and there is a wrong. The difference between them is the concern of ethics. We seek a way to find the right which is neither subjective nor arbitrary. We seek norms and principles which transcend prejudice or mere societal conventions. We seek an objective basis for our ethical standards. Ultimately we seek a knowledge of the character of God, whose holiness is to be reflected and mirrored in our patterns of behavior. With God there is a definite and absolute black and white. The problem for us is to discover which things belong where. The model below depicts our dilemma:

SIN   VIRTUE

The black section represents sin or unrighteousness. The white section represents virtue or righteousness. What does the gray represent? The gray area may call attention to two different problems of Christian ethics. It may be used to refer to those activities which the Bible describes as being *adiapherous*. Adiapherous matters refer to those things which in themselves are ethically neutral. Such matters as eating food offered to idols are placed in this category. In themselves adiapherous matters are not sin but there are occasions when they might become sin. Ping-Pong playing, for example, is not sin. But if a person becomes obsessed with Ping-Pong to the extent that it dominates his life, it becomes a sinful thing for that person.

However, the second problem of the gray area is more important for us to grasp. Here the gray area represents *confusion:* it encompasses those matters where we are uncertain about what is right and wrong. The presence of gray calls attention to the fact that ethics is not a simple science, but a complex one. Finding the black and the white areas is a noble concern—jumping to them simplistically, however, is devastating to the Christian life. When we react to black/white approaches to ethics, we may be accurately assessing an annoying human tendency toward simplistic thinking. We must guard against the reactionary posture of leaping to the conclusion that there are no limits of black and white. Only within the context of atheism can we speak of no black and white. We desire competent and consistent theism, which demands a rigorous scrutiny of ethical principles in order to find our way out of the confusion of the gray.

THE ETHICAL CONTINUUM

Our graph may also be used to illustrate the ethical continuum. In classical terms, sin is described as righteousness run amok. Evil is seen as the negation, privation, or distortion of the good. Man was created to labor in a garden. In modern jargon the workplace is described as a jungle. What is the difference between a garden and a jungle? A jungle is merely a chaotic garden, a garden run wild.

Man was created with an aspiration for significance, a virtue. Man can pervert that drive into a lust for power, a vice. These represent the two poles on the continuum. At some point we pass over a line between virtue and vice. The closer we come to that line, the more difficult it is for us to perceive it clearly and the more our minds encounter the fogginess of gray.

In teaching a course on ethics to clergymen working on Doctor of Ministry degrees, I posed the following ethical dilemma:

Suppose a husband and wife are interned in a concentration camp. They are housed in separate quarters with no communication between them. A guard approaches the wife and demands that she have sexual intercourse with him. The wife refuses.

The guard then declares that unless the woman submits to his overtures, he will have her husband shot. The woman submits. When the camp is liberated and the husband learns of his wife's behavior, he sues her for divorce on the grounds of adultery. I then posed this question to twenty conservative clergymen: "Would you grant the man a divorce on the grounds of adultery?" All twenty answered "yes," pointing to the obvious fact that the wife did have sexual relations with the guard. They saw extenuating circumstances in the situation, but the situation did not change the fact of the wife's immoral behavior.

I then asked, "If a woman is forcibly raped, may the husband sue for divorce on the grounds of adultery?" All twenty responded, "no." The clergymen all recognized a clear distinction between adultery and rape. The difference is found at the point of coercion versus voluntary participation. I pointed out that the prison guard used coercion (forcible compliance lest the husband be killed) and asked if the woman's "adultery" was not actually rape.

With the mere raising of the question half of the clergymen changed their verdict. After prolonged discussion almost all of them did. The presence of the element of coercion threw the adultery issue into the gray area of confusion. Even those who did not completely change their verdict strongly modified it to account for the extenuating circumstances which moved the woman's "crime" from the clear area of sin into the gray area of complexity. They all agreed that if it was sin, it was a lesser sin than adultery committed with "malice aforethought."

That a continuum exists between virtue and vice

was the main thrust of Jesus' teaching in the Sermon on the Mount. He was teaching the principle of the complex of righteousness and the complex of sin. The Pharisees had embraced a simplistic understanding of the Ten Commandments. Their ethical judgments were superficial and therefore distorted. They failed to grasp the continuum motif.

Recently I read an article by a prominent psychiatrist who was critical of Jesus' ethical teaching. He expressed astonishment that the western world had been so laudatory about Jesus as a "great teacher." He pointed to the Sermon on the Mount as exhibit A for the foolishness of Jesus' ethical teaching. He asked why we extol the wisdom of a teacher who taught that it was just as bad for a man to lust after a woman as it is to commit adultery with her. He questioned how a teacher could argue that it was just as bad to be angry at a man or to call him a fool as it is to murder him. He then belabored the difference between the destruction caused by lust as opposed to adultery and that caused by slander as opposed to murder.

The answer to the psychiatrist should be clear. Jesus did not teach that lust was as bad as adultery, or that slander was as bad as murder. (Unfortunately, many Christians have jumped to the same erroneous conclusion as the psychiatrist, obscuring the point of Jesus' ethical teaching.)

Jesus was correcting the simplistic view of the law held by the Pharisees. They had embraced an "everything but" philosophy of technical morality, assuming that if they avoided the most obvious dimension of the Commandments, they had fulfilled the law. Like the Rich Young Ruler they had a simplistic and external understanding of the Decalogue. Because they had never actually murdered anyone, they thought they had kept the law perfectly. Jesus spelled out the wider implications or the complex of the law. "Thou shalt not kill" means more than refraining from homicide. It prohibits the entire complex that goes into murder. It implies its opposite virtue: "Thou shalt promote life." In our continuum, we see the following range:

VICE	VIRTUE
MURDER-HATRED-SLANDER	SAVING LIFE

A similar continuum moves from the virtue of chastity to the vice of adultery. In between are lesser virtues and lesser sins but sins nevertheless.

Slander doesn't kill the body or leave the wife a widow and the children orphans. It does destroy a man's good name, which robs him of a quality aspect of life. Slander murders the man "in spirit." Jesus' teaching is to reveal both the spirit and the letter of the law. The Pharisees had become crass literalists, ignoring the spirit of the law and missing the wider concerns of the complex of the sin of murder.

DEGREES OF SIN?

To speak of an ethical continuum or a complex of righteousness and evil is to plunge us into the debate over degrees of sin and righteousness. The Bible teaches that if we sin against one point of the law we sin against the whole law. Does this not imply that sin is sin and that ultimately there are no degrees? Has not Protestantism repudiated the Roman Catholic distinction between mortal and venial sins?

These are the issues which rage as soon as we begin to speak of degrees of sin. Certainly the Bible teaches that if we sin against one point of the law we sin against the whole law, but we must not infer from this that there are no degrees. Sinning against the law is in reality sinning against the God of the law. When I violate one point of God's law, I bring myself in opposition to God Himself. This is not to say that sinning against one point of the law is the equivalent of sinning against five points of the law. In both cases I violate the law and do violence to God, but the frequency of my violence is five times as great in the latter as in the former.

It is true that God commands perfect obedience to the whole law, so that by a single transgression I stand exposed to His judgment. The lightest sin exposes me to the wrath of God and in the smallest peccadillo I am guilty of cosmic treason. In the least transgression I set myself above the authority of God, doing insult to His majesty, His holiness, and His sovereign right to govern me. Sin is a revolutionary act in which the sinner seeks to depose God from His throne. Sin is a presumption of supreme arrogance in that the creature vaunts his own wisdom above that of the Creator, challenges divine omnipotence with human impotence, and seeks to usurp the rightful authority of the cosmic Lord.

It is true that historic Protestantism has rejected the Roman Catholic schema of mortal and venial sin. The rejection however, is not based on a rejection of degrees of gradations of sin. Calvin, for example, argued that all sin is mortal in the sense that it rightly deserves death, but that no sin is mortal in the sense that it destroys justifying grace. Considerations other than the degrees of sin were in view in the Protestant rejection of the mortal and venial sin distinction. Historic Protestantism retained the distinction between ordinary sins and sins which are deemed gross and heinous.

The most obvious reason for the Protestant retention of degrees of sin is that the Bible abounds with such gradations. The Old Testament law had clear distinctions and provisions of penalty for different levels of criminal acts. Some sins were punishable by death, others by corporal penalties, and still others by the levying of fines. In the Jewish criminal justice system, distinctions were made between types of murder which would correspond to modern-day distinctions such as first- and second-degree murder, and voluntary and involuntary manslaughter.

The New Testament lists certain sins that demand the forfeiture of Christian fellowship for the impenitent continuance of them. At the same time, the New Testament advocates a kind of love which covers a multitude of sins. Warnings abound concerning a future judgment which will take into account both the number (quantity) and the severity (quality) of our sins. Jesus speaks of those who will receive many stripes and those who will receive few; of the comparatively greater judgment that will befall Chorazim and Bethsaida as opposed to the judgment on Sodom and Gomorrah; and the greater and lesser degree of rewards that will be distributed to the saints. The Apostle Paul warns the Romans against heaping up wrath against the Day of Wrath. These and a host of other passages indicate that God's judgment will be perfectly just, measuring the number, the severity, and the extenuating circumstances which attend all of our sins.

TWO
REVEALED ETHICS

At the heart of Christian ethics is the conviction that our firm basis for knowing the true, the good, and the right is divine revelation. Christianity is not a life system which operates on the basis of speculative reason or pragmatic expediency. We assert boldly that God has revealed to us who He is, who we are, and how we are expected to relate to Him. He has revealed for us that which is pleasing to Him and commanded by Him. Revelation provides a supernatural aid in understanding the good. This point is so basic and so obvious that it has often been overlooked and obscured as we search for answers to particular questions.

The departure from divine revelation has brought our culture to chaos in the area of ethics. We have lost our basis of knowledge, our epistemological foundation, for discovering the good. This is not to suggest that God has given us a code book that is so detailed in its precepts that all ethical decisions become easy. That would be a vast oversimplification of the truth. God has not given us specific instructions for each and every possible ethical issue we face, but neither are we left to grope in the dark and make our decisions on the basis of pure opinion. This is an important comfort to the Christian, because when dealing with ethical questions we are never working in a vacuum. The ethical decisions that we make touch the lives of people and mold and shape human personality and character. It is precisely at this point that we need the assistance of the superiority of God's wisdom.

To be guided by God's revelation is both comforting and risky. It is comforting because we can rest in the assurance that our ethical decisions proceed from the mind of One whose wisdom is transcendent. God's law not only reflects His righteous character but also manifests His infinite wisdom. His knowledge of our humanity and His grasp of our needs for fullness of growth and development far exceed the collective wisdom of all of the world's greatest thinkers. Psychiatrists will never understand the human psyche to the degree the Creator understands that which He has made. God knows our frames; it is He who has made us so fearfully and wonderfully. All of the nuances and complexities that bombard our senses and coalesce to produce a human personality are known in their intimate details by the divine mind.

Taking comfort in divine revelation is risky business. It is risky precisely because the presence of hostility in the human heart to the rule of God makes for conflict between divine precepts and human desires. To take an ethical stand on the foundation of divine revelation is to bring one's self into serious and at times radical conflict with the opinions of men. Daily, clergymen in this nation give counsel and advice which runs contrary to the clear mandates of God. How can we explain such a hiatus between God's Word and ministerial counsel?

One critical factor in this dilemma is the fact that ministers are subjected to profound pressures of conformity to contemporary acceptable standards. The person who comes to the minister for counsel is not always looking for guidance from a transcendent God, but rather for permission to do what he or she wants. The Christian counselor is vulnerable to sophisticated forms of manipulation coming from the very people who seek his advice. So often what is desired is a license to sin and the minister is placed in that difficult pressure point of either acquiescing to the desires of the people or being considered unloving and fun-squelching. Add to this the cultural emphasis that there is something dehumanizing in discipline and moral restraints imposed upon us by God. Thus, to stand with God is often to stand against men and to face the fiery trials that go with such convictions.

Ethics involves the question of authority. The Christian lives under the sovereignty of God, who alone may claim sovereignty over us. Christian ethics is theocentric as opposed to secular or philosophical ethics which tends to be anthropocentric. For the humanist, man is the norm, the ultimate standard of behavior. Christians, however, assert that God is the center of all things and that His character is the absolute standard by which questions of right and wrong are determined.

The sovereignty of God deals not only with abstract principles but with real lines of authority. God has the right to issue commands, to impose obligations, and to bind the consciences of men. Christians live in the context of theonomy. Debates about law and ethics tend to focus on two basic options, autonomy and heteronomy. Autonomy declares that man is a law unto himself. The autonomous man creates his own value system, establishes his own norms, and is answerable and accountable to man and to man alone. Heteronomy means "ruled by another." In any system of heteronomy, the individual is considered to be morally responsible to obey limits and proscriptions imposed upon him by someone else. This someone else might be another individual, a group such as the state, or even a transcendent God. When we speak of theonomy, or the rule of God, we are distinguishing a specific kind of heteronomy. Theonomy is rule by another who is identified as God. This distinction between autonomy and theonomy is the most fundamental conflict of mankind. When theonomy surrenders to autonomy, the biblical description of that surrender is sin. It is the creature's declaration of independence from his Creator.

There is an important difference between freedom and autonomy. Though autonomy is a kind of freedom, it carries the dimensions of freedom to the level of the absolute. Christianity asserts that man is given freedom by God, but that his freedom has limits. Our freedom never moves us to the point of autonomy. Some have viewed the fall of man in Eden as a result of man's primordial grasp for autonomy—man's basal sin, the attempt to usurp the authority that belongs to God.

Friedrich Nietzsche, in trying to locate the most basic of human characteristics, located it in what he called man's lust or will to power. For Nietzsche the authentic man is the one who creates his own values and refuses to submit to the herd morality of the masses. He postulates an existential hero who has the courage to create his own values. For man to create his own values absolutely, the first thing he must do is to declare the death of God. As long as God exists, He represents the ultimate threat to man's pretended autonomy. Jean-Paul Sartre addresses this theme in declaring that unless freedom reaches the full measure of autonomy, it is not true freedom. Thus Sartre too must stand with those who would dismiss God from the area of ethics.

Our concept of liberty has changed drastically from eighteenth-century America to twentieth-century America. The change has much to do with our understanding of autonomy. The quest for autonomy is considered by modern man to be a noble and virtuous declaration of human creativity. From the Christian vantage point, however, the quest for autonomy represents the essence of evil as it contains within its agenda the assassination of God.

The contemporary existentialist cries that "cowering in the shadow of the Almighty" is the worst thing man can do. Such human dependency upon divine assistance, he says, encourages weakness and inevitable decadence. To be sure, many people flee to Christianity because of moral weakness, but the fundamental issue is not what we regard to be preferable states of mind or psychological attitudes. The ultimate issue centers on the existence of God. It matters not whether I enjoy submitting to God. What matters first is the question, "Is there a God?" Without God the only possible end of ethical reflection is chaos. Dostoevski said, "If there is no God, all things are permissible."

The God of Christianity is sovereign, wise, righteous, and ultimately concerned with justice. Not only is God concerned with justice, but He assumes the role of Judge over us. It is axiomatic to Christianity that our actions will be judged. This theme is conspicuously absent in much Christian teaching today, yet it fills the New Testament and touches virtually every sermon of Jesus of Nazareth. We will be called into account for every idle word we speak. On the final day it is not *our* consciences which will accuse or excuse us, but the conscience of God.

Christian ethics is not established in a vacuum. The Christian is not concerned with ethics for ethics' sake. We understand that rules for conduct are established in the context of God's will for human redemption. There is a real sense in which grace precedes law. The very giving of commandments by the Creator is in the context of a covenant which God makes on the basis of grace. The purpose of divine commandments is redemption. The law of the Old Testament and of the New Testament is fundamentally person-oriented. To isolate this law from its basic concern for persons is to fall into the abyss of legalism. Christian ethics is built upon obedience of persons to a personal God. When God first gave the law, He did so by means of a personal introduction: "*I* am the Lord *your* God; *you* are *my* people. Therefore, you shall not. . . ." We see that this is not law for law's sake, but for people's sake.

THREE
LEGALISM AND ANTINOMIANISM

The continuum of ethics is divided sharply by a fine line, the razor's edge. This fine line of demarcation is similar to what Jesus described as the "narrow way." The New Testament makes frequent reference to Christians living according to "the way." Christians in the first century were called "people of the way." Jesus called His disciples to walk by the narrow way and enter by the straight gate that leads to life, while warning against the broad way that leads to destruction. There is a difference between a narrow way and narrow-mindedness. Narrow-mindedness reveals a judgmental attitude, a critical mind set, which is far from the biblical ideal of charity. Walking the narrow way involves not a distorted mental attitude, but a clear focus of what righteousness demands.

31

One can deviate from the path of righteousness by moving too far to the left or to the right. One can stumble from the narrow way by falling off the road in either direction. If we consider ethics again in terms of the model of the continuum, we know that the opposite poles which represent distortions of authentic righteousness may be labled legalism and antinomianism. These twin distortions have plagued the church as long as it has been in existence. The New Testament documents reflect that struggles with both legalism and antinomianism were common in the New Testament church.

Legalism is a distortion that takes many forms. The first form of legalism involves the abstracting of the law of God from its original context. This variety of legalism reduces Christianity to a list of do's and don'ts, a codified system of rigid moralism that is divorced from the covenant context of love. To be sure, God gives rules. He pronounces do's and don'ts, but the purpose of these rules is to describe for us what is pleasing and displeasing to God. God is concerned with the attitude of the heart that one brings with him to the application of the rules. When the rules are kept for their own sake, then obedience is given to a cold abstraction known as the law rather than to a personal God who reveals the law.

A second dimension of legalism, closely related to the first, involves the divorce of the letter of the law from the spirit of the law. This was the distortion Jesus dealt with constantly with the Pharisees and it was rebuked by our Lord's teachings in the Sermon on the Mount. As we have indicated with respect to Jesus' expansion of the full import of the law in the

Sermon on the Mount, it is not enough for the godly person to obey the mere externals of the law while ignoring the deeper implications of the spirit behind the law. The Pharisees became masters of external obedience coupled with internal disobedience.

The difference between spirit and letter touches the question of motive. When the Bible describes goodness, it does so in a complex way. Some are offended by the universal indictment brought against fallen mankind which Paul articulates in his epistle to the Romans. The Apostle declares that "none is righteous, no not one; there is none who does good." Here the Apostle echoes the radical statement with which Jesus replied to the question of the Rich Young Ruler: "Why callest thou me good? Only God is good." At face value, the Bible seems to teach that no one ever does a good thing in this world. This is a grim evaluation of the conduct of fallen human beings.

How are we to understand this radical judgment of human ethical conduct? The key is to be found in an analysis of the biblical definition of the good. For an action to be judged good by God, it must fulfill two primary requirements. The first is that the action outwardly corresponds to the demands of the law. In addition, the inward motivation is also considered by God. The motive for the act must proceed from a heart that is altogether disposed toward the glory of God. It is the second dimension, the spiritual dimension of motive, which disqualifies so many of our deeds from the evaluation of being good. A pagan, a person of profound corruption, may do acts which externally conform to the demands of the law. The internal motivation, however, is that of selfish interest or what the theologians call "enlightened self-interest," a motive which is not in harmony with the great commandment. Our external deeds may measure up to the external demands of the law while, at the same time, our hearts are far removed from God.

Consider the example of a person driving his automobile within the context of legal speed limits. A person goes on a trip from one city to another, passing along the way a diversity of zones with differing speed limits. For cruising on the highway, the speed limit is established at fifty-five miles an hour; for moving through a suburban community's school zone, the speed limit drops to fifteen miles an hour. Suppose our driver has a preference for operating his vehicle at a speed of fifty-five miles an hour. He drives consistently at the speed he prefers. While driving on the highway, his activity is observed by policemen who note that he is driving in exact conformity to the requirements of the law, giving the appearance of the model safe driver and the upstanding and obedient citizen. He is obeying the law, however, not because he has a concern for the safety and well-being of others or out of a motive to be civilly obedient, but rather because he simply happens to enjoy driving his car at fifty-five miles an hour. This preference is noted when his car moves into the school zone and he keeps the accelerator pressed down, maintaining the speed of fifty-five miles an hour. Now, as he executes his preference, he becomes a clear and present danger, indeed a menace to children walking in the school zone. He is moving at a speed of forty miles an hour over the speed limit. His external obedience to the law vanishes when the law conflicts with his own desires.

The difference between our perception and God's is that our ability is limited to the observation of external modes of behavior. God can perceive the heart; God alone knows the deepest motives and intentions that undergird our practice and behavior. Legalism is concerned simply with external conformity and is blind to internal motivation.

Perhaps the most deadly and most widespread form of legalism is that type which adds legislation to the law of God and treats it as if it were divine law. The Old Testament prophets expressed God's fury at this form of behavior, lamenting the result of "binding men where God had left them free." It is a manifestation of man's fallenness to impose his own sense of propriety on other people, seeking mass conformity to his own preferences and adding insult to it by declaring these prejudices and preferences to be nothing less than the will of God. A frequent point of conflict between Jesus and the Pharisees centered on the Pharisees' traditions, which imposed hardships on the people who were bound by these man-made obligations. The rebuke attacked the Pharisees because they had elevated their traditions to the level of the law of God, seeking not only to usurp God's authority, but to oppress mankind.

The elevation of human preferences to the level of divine mandate is not limited to an isolated group of moralistic Pharisees in the first century. The problem has beset the church ever since. Not only do traditions develop which are added to the law of God, but in many cases they become the supreme tests of the faith, the litmus test by which people are judged to be either Christians or non-Christians. It is unthinkable in the New Testament that a person's Christian commitment would ever be determined by whether or not that person engaged in dancing, or in wearing of lipstick and the like. Unfortunately, so often when these preferences become tests of faith, they involve not only the elevation of non-biblical mandates to the level of the will of God, but they represent the trivialization of righteousness. When these externals are elevated to the level of being measuring rods of righteousness, we begin to major in minors and obscure the real tests of righteousness.

Closely related to the elevation of human traditions to the norm of law is the problem of majoring in minors which again was modeled negatively by the Pharisees. The Pharisees distorted the emphasis of biblical righteousness to suit their own behavioral patterns of self-justification. Frequently Jesus critiques the Pharisees at this point. Jesus says to them, "You tithe your mint and your cummin, but you omit the weightier matters of the law, justice and mercy." On numerous occasions Jesus acknowledges that some points of the law were scrupulously obeyed by the Pharisees. They paid their tithes, they read their Bible, they did a host of things which the law required—and Jesus commended them for their actions, saying, "These things you ought to have done." However it was the emphasis that was out of kilter. They scrupulously tithed, but in doing so they used their obedience to this lesser matter as a cloak to cover up their refusal to obey the weightier matters of justice and mercy. That distortion occurs today.

Why do we have a perpetual struggle of majoring in minors? Certainly we as Christians want to be recognized for our growth in sanctification and for our righteousness. Which is easier to achieve, a mature level of the practice of mercy and righteousness, or the paying of tithes? To pay my tithes certainly involves a financial sacrifice of sorts, but there is a certain sense in which it is cheaper for me to drop my money into the plate than it is for me to invest my life in the pursuit of justice and of mercy. We tend to give God the cheapest gifts. Which is easier, to develop the gift of the fruits of the Spirit, conquering pride and coveteousness, greed and impatience, or to avoid going to movie theaters or dancing? We also yearn for clearly observable measuring rods of growth. How do we measure our growth in patience or in compassion? It is much more difficult to measure the disposition of our hearts than it is to measure the number of movies we attend.

It is also our inclination as fallen creatures to emphasize as being most important those virtues in which we have achieved a relative degree of success. Naturally, I would like to think that my moral strong points are the important ones and my moral weaknesses are limited to minor matters. It is a short step from this natural inclination to a widespread distortion of where God places the emphasis.

One final type of legalism is what we call "loopholeism." Loopholeism involves getting around the law by legal and moral technicalities. Again we return to the Pharisees for the biblical model of loopholeism. The Pharisees had a clearly defined tradition about restrictions of travel on the Sabbath day. One was not permitted to travel more than a "Sabbath day's journey," which was defined by so many miles from one's home, on the Sabbath. If a Pharisee wanted to travel a distance which exceeded these limits, he would take advantage of a technical provision in the law to establish residence during the week. He would have a traveling merchant take some articles of clothing or possessions such as toothbrushes and put them on strategic points along the road. Perhaps at the two-mile mark the Pharisee's toothbrush would be placed under a rock, thereby legally establishing "residence" at that rock. Now, with his legal residences defined in two-mile increments along the way, the Pharisee was free to travel from rock to rock—from "residence to residence"—and make his full trip without ever covering more than the prescribed distance from his home. Here the Sabbath-day journey principle was violated shamefully while technically being protected by the loophole.

In the decade of the sixties, Gail Green wrote a book describing the sexual behavior patterns of the American college woman. Dr. Green maintained that the prevalent ethical principle at that time was the "everything but" philosophy. Many forms of sexual activity were considered legitimate as long as the woman stopped short of actual intercourse. It seems almost naive today to think of a generation of college students who embraced an "everything but" philosophy, as those lines have fallen away since that earlier period. The mentality of the "everything but" philosophy is an example of technical loopholeism where a person could be a virgin in the technical sense yet be involved in all sorts of premarital and extramarital sexual acts.

As legalism distorts the biblical ethic in one direction, so the opposite pole is the distortion of antinomianism. Antinomianism simply means "anti-lawism." As legalism comes in many shapes and sizes, so there are subtle forms of antinomianism which also may be delineated. We are living in a period in Christian history where antinomianism is rampant in the church.

The first type of antinomianism is libertinism, the idea that the Christian is no longer bound to obedience to the law of God in any way. This view of the law is often linked with the cardinal Protestant doctrine, justification by faith alone. In this view one understands justification by faith to mean that after a Christian is converted, he is no longer liable in any sense to fulfill the commandments of the law. He sees his justification as a license to sin, excusing himself by arguing that he lives by grace and not by law and is under no obligation to maintain the commandments of God.

It was the fear of such a distortion of the biblical concept of justification that was expressed by Roman Catholic theologians in the 16th century. They feared that Luther's insistence on justification by faith alone would open a floodgate of iniquity by those who would understand the doctrine in precisely these terms. The Lutheran movement was quick to point out that though justification is by faith alone, it is by a kind of faith which is not alone.

Unless the believer's sanctification is evidenced by true conformity to the commandments of Christ, it is certain that no authentic justification ever really took place. Jesus stated it this way, "If you love me, keep my commandments." Christ is a commandment-giving Lord. If one has true justifying faith, he moves diligently to pursue the righteousness of obedience which Christ demands.

A second type of antinomianism may be called "gnostic spiritualism." The early gnostics, believing they had a monopoly on spiritual knowledge, plagued the Christian community. They claimed to be people "in the know," taking their name from the Greek word *Gnosis,* which means "knowledge." They claimed a superior sort of mystical knowledge that gave them the right to sidestep or supplant the mandates given to the Christian community by the apostolic word. Though gnosticism as a formal doctrine has passed from the scene, many subtle varieties of this ancient heresy persist to this day. Evangelical Christians frequently fall into the trap of claiming that the Spirit of God leads them to do things that are clearly contrary to the written Word of God. I have had Christians come to me and report behavioral patterns that violated the commandments of Christ, but then say, "I prayed about this and feel at peace in the matter." Some have indeed committed outrage to the Spirit of truth and of holiness by not only seeking to excuse their transgressions by appealing to some mystical sense of peace delivered to them by the Holy Ghost, but by actually laying the blame for the impulse of their sin at the feet of God the Holy Spirit. This comes perilously close to blasphemy against the Holy Spirit and certainly lies within the boundaries of grieving the Holy Spirit. The Spirit of God agrees with the Word of God. The Spirit of God is not an antinomian.

A third example of antinomianism which has made a profound impact on the Christian community in the twentieth century is the rise of situational ethics. Situational ethics is frequently known by another label, the "new morality." To identify this theory with one single individual would be a distortion. Dietrich Bonhoeffer's work on *Ethics,* Brunner's *The Divine Imperative,* Paul Lehmann's *Ethics in a Christian Context,* all have contributed to situational ethics. Bishop John A. T. Robinson of *Honest to God* fame and Bishop Pike have also entered this discussion. But Joseph Fletcher, in *Situation Ethics,* has done more to popularize this theory than anyone else.

"There are times when a man has to push his principles aside and do the right thing." This St. Louis cabbie's remark is indicative of the style and mood of Fletcher's book. "You're so full of what's right, you can't see what's good." This is the Texas rancher's remark in *The Rainmaker.* He is the co-hero of Fletcher's book.

The general basis for situation ethics is that there is one and only one absolute, normative ethical principle to which every human being is bound— the law of love, a law which is not always easy to discern. Fletcher realized that the word "love" is "a swampy one."

Fletcher argues that there are three basic approaches to ethical decision-making: legalism, antinomianism, and situationism. Legalism he defines as a preoccupation with the letter of the law. The principles of law are not merely guidelines or principles to illuminate a given situation; they are directives to be followed absolutely, pre-set solutions, and you can "look them up in a book." He charges that Judaism, Roman Catholicism, and Classical Protestantism have been legalistic in this sense. He points to such episodes of crass legalism in church history as the burning of homosexuals at the stake during the Middle Ages. Also in the Old Testament homosexuals were subject to the death penalty.

Antinomianism has no regard for law. Every decision is purely existential. Moral decisions are made in a random and spontaneous fashion. Fletcher sees that the legalist has too many maxims and the antinomian has none. He maintains that situationism is a middle ground for a more workable ethic. The situationist treats with respect the traditional principles of his heritage, but he is always prepared to set them aside if, in that situation, love seems better served by doing so.

Fletcher distinguishes between principles and rules: principles *guide,* rules *direct.* In working out the application of applying the law of love, he sets up working principles which serve as the guidelines:

1. Pragmatism—the good and the true is determined by that which works.
2. Relativism—the situationist avoids words like "never," "always," "perfect," and "absolutely." (The basic drift of secular man is to deny the existence of any absolutes. Fletcher asserts that there is one absolute as a reference point for a "normative relativism.")
3. Positivism—particularized, *ad hoc,* to-the-

point principles. The situationist is not looking for universals; his affirmations are posited, not deduced. Faith propositions are affirmed voluntarily rather than rationally, being more acts of the will than of the mind. We cannot prove our concept of love. The end product of our ethic is a decision, not a conclusion.

4. Personalism—ethics deal with human relationships. The legalist is a "what-asker": what does the law say? The situationist is a "who-asker": who is to be helped? The emphasis is on people rather than on ideas or principles in the abstract.

We still have the question, "What do we ask ourselves to discover what love demands in a given situation? How do we protect ourselves from a distorted view of love?" Fletcher offers four questions to consider.

1. The end: for what result are we aiming?
2. Means: how may we secure this end?
3. Motive: why is that our aim?
4. Consequences: what forseeably might happen?

All of these need to be considered before an ethical decision can be made.

There are some positive aspects about this system of situation ethics, as some of the principles involved are commendable. First, situation ethics is not absolute relativism. It is a normative ethic, a kind of absolutism. The limitation to *one* absolute facilitates decision-making and eliminates a certain paralysis of the man who is considering many absolutes.

One of the first insights of situation ethics is that it emphasizes that ethical decisions do not take place in a vacuum. They are made in a very real and often painful context. That context should be considered. The high value placed on love and on the worth of persons is also a commendable trait of this position.

All these considered, however, there are still some serious inadequacies to this approach. What underlies the debate between orthodoxy and the situational ethicist is the question of the normativity of God's revelation in Scripture.

Fletcher oversimplifies the distinctions between and the definition of legalism, antinomianism, and situationalism. Legalism is a distortion of absolutism. Even Fletcher is an absolutist, though with just one absolute, and all of the legalistic dangers of absolutism are present in his system. One could easily legalistically obey the law of love. If this law is divorced from his context, legalism could easily emerge.

Why, when one holds more than one absolute, is the charge of legalism leveled? Haven't the situationists been simplistic and reductionistic in arbitrarily choosing love as the only absolute? God has laid more than one absolute requirement upon man. There is nothing in reason *or* revelation that would cause one to isolate love as the only absolute. When questioned, these men appeal to Scripture and the teachings of Jesus and Paul. But they are quite selective about their appeal to Scripture, falling into the quandary of the ethically arbitrary.

Related to this, the most serious deficiency of Fletcher's system is the problem of how we determine what love demands. We agree with the principle that one should do what love demands. But Fletcher has problems in determining these demands. Certainly the Bible teaches us to do what love commands, and the content of love is defined by God's revelation. Doing what love demands is the same as saying, "Do what God commands." If we obeyed the Scriptures like a sterile book of rules, we would be legalists. But if we see the Bible as being the revelation of the One who is Love, then we must take seriously what Love has commanded.

When we are left to make an ethical decision, knowing that we are fallen; knowing that we are given over to vices; knowing that we can never perfectly read our own motives; knowing that we are limited to forseeable consequences; knowing that we can never comprehensively analyze the ends and the means; knowing all these things, we have a very precarious situation on our hands *if* we have rejected the Bible as normative revelation. God has not left us to make these decisions with unaided reason.

In Ephesians 5:1, we are given an imperative to be followers of God:

Be ye therefore followers of God as dear children: and walk in love, as Christ also hath loved us, and hath given himself for us an offering and a sacrifice to God for a sweetsmelling savour. But fornication, and all uncleanness, or covetousness, let it not once be named among you, as becoming saints.

Here the biblical ethic is on a collision course with

situationism. To be a follower of God is an absolute. At no point, in no situation, are we permitted to leave off the following of God. We are to walk in love, the kind of love embodied in the sacrificial ministry of Christ. Love stands here as an absolute— a norm. Its absolute call upon us, however, is not left entirely to the situation, informed by more "guides." The Apostle immediately adds an absolute application to it involving fornication, uncleanness, and covetousness. He says, "Let it *not once* be named among you. . . ." Paul falls into Fletcher's definition of legalism by making a universal prohibition. The Apostle falls into the absolute realm of the "never."

Situationism stops with the injunction to walk in love. It must then allow for certain situations where fornication is not only permitted but preferred. If love "demands it" in a given situation, then fornication must be practiced. How perilous is this "guideline," particularly in light of man's most ancient ploy of seduction, "If you love me, you will . . . ."

It is difficult to conceive of concrete situations in which idolatry would be virtuous or coveting an expression of love. Paul concludes his admonition with a caveat:

Let no man deceive you with vain words: for because of these things cometh the wrath of God upon the children of disobedience.

Situationism makes the precepts of God relative, leaving us with the mandate to walk in love but to figure it out for ourselves by means of the guidelines of pragmatism, relativism, positivism, and personalism. At this point situationism is exposed as a virulent form of antinomianism masquerading as a legitimate option between legalism and antinomianism. We cannot realistically expect legalists to call themselves legalists or antinomians to plead their guilt before the world. Though Fletcher protests to the contrary, the substantive elements of antinomianism are rife in his thought.

The Christian ethicist asserts that not only does the Bible require us to do what love demands, but that it reveals quite precisely at times what it is that love demands. We have directive content in the Scriptures. We are not left with illuminators, but with divine commands.

Consider certain of the Ten Commandments from the standpoint of situationism:

"Thou shalt have no other gods before me," unless it would seem in some situation to be the loving thing to do.

"Thou shalt not make any graven images" unless, on the basis of foreseeable ends, means, motives and consequences, love would be best served by making graven images. Consider Daniel's dilemma in the lions' den. He could have refrained from praying to God. Certainly the people needed his leadership. What good would he do God's people in the lions' den? Should he sell out the people and leave them without God's agent of revelation for a simple principle of prayer? The end that he wants is survival. His means are to obey the king. His motive is to serve the people of God. The foreseeable consequences would be that some people might be disappointed but he would be able to make up for that by being a leader and guide to them. So Daniel should receive the blessing of God for doing the loving thing and abstain from prayer to his God.

One of the uniquenesses of the true people of God is not legalism, but fidelity, trust, and obedience to God. Obeying the law to love God is not legalism. When we consider Christ's obedience to God and to the law, it seems impossible not to regard situationism as a serious heretical distortion of the biblical ethic.

There is a principle in the biblical ethic that is rarely seen in the writings of the situationists. They fail to emphasize, as does the Bible, that doing what love demands, what Christ commands, often means the bearing of unspeakable suffering. It means to participate in radical humiliation and to count one's life as nothing for the exaltation of Christ. It may mean spending a life rotting in a cell in a concentration camp rather than to violate the commandment of Christ.

Christ's statement about love is our norm: "If you love me, keep my commandments." The proof of our love is obedience to Christ's commandments. Situation ethics establishes a false dichotomy between love and obedience. Situation ethics fails because it does not take love seriously enough.

We turn our attention now to specific questions of ethics which have become particularly controversial in our times, glancing briefly at questions of materialism, capital punishment, war, and abortion.

FOUR
THE ETHICS
OF MATERIALISM

Materialism has become a controversial issue in the church today, expecially with the emergence of Christian youth movements. Several groups have made this a central issue of debate, speaking of materialism not in the metaphysical sense, but rather in the economic sense: "That world view which places the accumulation of material things at the zenith of private and corporate concern." The pursuit of wealth is seen as the highest good in materialism. Materialism can be distinguished from its opposite, which might be called "spiritualism" or (better) "idealism," which sees that only spiritual values are worthy of human pursuit.

The biblical position repudiates both of these positions. Though material things are not the highest good, neither are they intrinsically evil. There is no room for radical asceticism or monasticism in the church, as these positions are world denying and creation denying. It is important to recognize that in the Old Covenant and in the New, many of God's redemptive promises relate to creation—promises of redemption of the physical world. The promise to Abraham and to his seed includes at its heart the promise of land and the promise of prosperity.

The principle of private property is pivotal to discussions of materialism. Many have argued that some kind of communal living or equal distribution of wealth is the only acceptable Christian norm, based on the presupposition that the concept of private property is illegitimate for the Christian. However, the concept of private property is inseparably related to the Creation Ordinance that sanctifies labor. Karl Marx did something of inestimable and lasting value for the history of the development of thought for Western man by making it impossible to conceive of the history of man without considering man's labor and the fruit of his labor as having influenced his development greatly. This is not to endorse Marxism but to recognize the crucial relationship between man and his labor. When man involves himself in labor, he involves himself with his responsibility of being made in the image of God.

The sanctity of labor is first of all instituted by the labor of God Himself in Creation. Labor, in Creation is a duty and a blessing, not a curse. The curse that is attached to labor after the fall has to do with the quality of work and the difficulty of our labor by which we bring forth fruit. The thorns and the sweat, not the work itself, are the curse. Pre-fall man existed in a condition where he labored, and that labor produced fruit which he had the right to enjoy.

Even after the fall, we have no indication that private property (the fruit of one's labor) is condemned or prohibited by God. Indeed, the first liturgical acts observed in the Old Testament are the presenting of offerings by Cain and Abel. Notice that their offering is validated in that it belongs to the one who offered it. The offertory system of the Old Testament makes no sense when divorced from the system of private property. One of the basic stipulations of making an offering is that you present something which belongs to you. This right of human ownership is something God has assigned as part of our covenant partnership with Him in creation. Though all ownership is answerable to divine ownership in the long run, this does not invalidate the concept of private property.

Examining the Decalogue, we see that private property is assumed in several situations. The prohibition against stealing presupposes private property, as does the prohibition against covetousness.

In terms of the relationship between labor and property, we gain an important insight by examining the Sabbath commandment. One of the things that is often overlooked is that not only does the commandment concern itself with the seventh day, but also with the first six. "Six days shalt thou labor...." The day of rest makes no sense apart from the six days of labor which precede it. The sanctity of labor is the ground-basis for private property. In both the Old and New Covenants, the call to labor is an emphatic one, bringing fruit as its just reward. The avoidance of labor is regarded as sin. Paul commands labor as an ethical norm. Idleness has no place in the New Testament ethic. In 2 Thessalonians 3:12, Paul says that persons should "earn their own living." In 1 Timothy 5:8, Paul adds that lack of provision for one's household makes one worse than an unbeliever.

There are two important conclusions to be drawn from these statements. First, there is the right of private property as the fruit of one's labor. Second, there is the responsibility of *honest* and *diligent* labor. Because we live to the glory of God, we have the responsibility to render an "honest day's labor." Our labor must not be for the simple end of the acquisition of wealth, but it should be for the glory of God.

This raises the problem of wealth, that is, the accumulation of material goods beyond the level of necessity. Are we permitted to earn and keep more than we need? We are indeed. The possession of wealth is nowhere condemned in either Old Testament or New Testament. The means of acquiring wealth are clearly regulated: exploitation, fraud, dishonesty, oppression, and power politics are all condemned. Prosperity and wealth are seen as an aspect of God's providence. This is one of the reasons why covetousness is such a weighty matter. When I covet, I am protesting against God's distribution of wealth. Abraham was perhaps one of the richest men in antiquity. Noah and Job were both wealthy men. Not only does God never condemn this wealth, but he legitimizes the passing of the wealth from generation to generation by means of inheritance. The patriarchal blessings, which pass on the material blessings, are part of the Messianic redemptive promise, including the promise of land.

In the New Testament we encounter wealthy men who are praiseworthy. Note the care of the body of Christ, after the Crucifixion, by Joseph of Arimathea, obviously a man of means.

What the New Testament says is that wealth imposes severe temptations. Jesus' statement about the camel going through the gate of Jerusalem, "the eye of the needle," indicates that a rich man who would enter heaven faces a huge task. Practically speaking, the maintenance and protection of wealth takes time and concentrated energy. The parable of the Rich Fool illustrates the perils of preoccupation with riches. It is easy for the rich man to confuse his priorities. It is also easy for the poor man. It is not merely the rich who are susceptible to the siren call of materialism; its seductive power crosses all of the socioeconomic borders.

What about the Christian's responsibility to the poor? This, of course, touches the heart of the matter of materialism. Obviously, the provision for the needs of the poor is a Christian responsibility. In the Old Testament the needs of the poor were met somewhat by the poor laws which included provisions for gleaners. The principle of bringing offerings to the needy is a practice enjoined by both Covenants. The collection of provisions by the Gentile Christians for famine-struck Jerusalem was one of the most notable and dramatic episodes in the first century. Both the Corinthian and the Philippian churches are praised by Paul for their generosity. The interesting thing is that the need was prophesied and a relief fund established in advance.

The principle of alms-giving is important to both Covenants. When my brother is in need, I must attempt to meet that need.

WHO ARE THE POOR?

"The poor you always have with you." This statement by Jesus has been taken by some as a license to neglect the poor as if Jesus were saying, "Oh, well, we always have poverty in our midst, so don't worry about it." Jesus recognized the perpetual plight of the poor, not to ignore it, but to call the Christian community to constant diligence in dealing with the problem.

In identifying the "poor" described in the Bible we can distinguish at least four different major categories of "poor" people. What follows is a brief description of these groups.

1. The Poor As a Result of Slothfulness. The Bible speaks of those who are poor because they are lazy, refusing to work. This indolent group receives sharp criticism from God and comes under His holy judgment. Karl Barth listed sloth as one of the primary and foundational sins of man, along with pride and dishonesty. It is to the slothful that God says, "Consider the ant, thou sluggard," shaming the lazy by telling them to go to insects for instruction. It is this group Paul undoubtedly has in mind when he says, "If a man does not work, neither should he eat."

Since the Bible does criticize the lazy poor, some have jumped to the conclusion that indolence and poverty are synonymous. Some assume that poverty is always and everywhere a sign of sloth. Thus the poor can be righteously shunned as they are left to suffer their "just penalty for sloth." Such attitudes reflect a woeful ignorance of or callous disregard for distinctions the Bible forces us to make. There are other reasons for poverty.

2. The Poor As a Result of Calamity. The Scriptures recognize that many are left in poverty because of the ravages of disease or disasters. The man born blind or the person left crippled by an accident, the farmer whose crops have been destroyed by flood or drought, all have just cause for their impoverished estate. These people are victims of circumstances not of their own making. For these "poor" the Bible adopts an attitude of compassion and genuine charity. It is the responsibility of the people of God to see to it that the suffering of these people is ameliorated. They are to be a priority concern of the Church. These are the hungry who are to be fed, the naked who are to be clothed.

3. The Poor As a Result of Exploitation. This group of poor are also oppressed. These are the masses who are frustrated daily by their inability to "fight city hall," the ones who live out the mournful slogan, "the rich get richer and the poor get poorer." This group suffers indignities when they live in societies where the social and political institutions, and especially the judicial systems favor the rich and the powerful and leave the poor without advocacy. Such was the condition of eighth-century-B.C. Israel when God thundered against His people. The Word of God came via prophetic criticism that demanded justice and righteousness in a time when the poor were being "sold for a pair of shoes." This was Israel's status when in bondage to Egypt. This kind of poverty moves God Himself as He hears the cries and groans of His oppressed people and says, "Let My people go!" Such injustice and inequity should always "move" God's Church. This is the Church's basis for necessary and legitimate social action.

4. *The Poor As a Result of Personal Sacrifice.* These poor people are designated by the New Testament as being poor "for righteousness' sake." This group, whose chief representative is Jesus Himself, is made up of people who are voluntarily poor. Their poverty is a result of a conscious decision to choose lifestyles or vocations with little or no financial remuneration. This class of poor is promised special blessings from God. They are poor because the priorities of their lives may not mesh with the value standards of the culture in which they live. It is Edwards, writing in almost microscopic print in order to conserve paper because of his meager stipend (ultimately costing the Church and universities hundreds of thousands of dollars to retrieve and reconstruct the priceless treasures of his words); it is Luther, forgoing a promising and lucrative career to wear the habit of the monk; it is the modern businessman who passes up the windfall deal because he has scruples about hidden unethical elements.

What can we learn from those four designations? In the first instance we should be warned not to lump all the poor together in one package. We must resist the tendency to generalize about poverty. An equally insistent warning must be voiced about the same kind of unjust grouping together of the rich. It would be slanderous to maintain that all rich people are corrupt, as if all riches were achieved through evil means or through exploiting the poor. Not all rich people are avaricious or ruthless. To indict the rich indiscriminately would be to condemn the likes of Abraham, Job, David, and Joseph of Arimathea.

Second, we must avoid a theological glamorizing of poverty. Throughout Church history there have been repeated efforts to make poverty the precondition for entrance to the Kingdom. It has been seen as a form of works righteousness whereby the poor have an automatic ticket into heaven. This substitutes justification by poverty for justification by faith.

Third, we must recognize that God cares deeply about human poverty and the consequent suffering. Our duty is to be no less concerned than God Himself. As long as the poor are with us, we are called to minister to them, not only via charity but by seeking and working for the reformation of social and political structures which enslave, oppress, and exploit.

The basic principle regarding wealth is the principle of stewardship, that a man is responsible for what he does with what he receives. He is not called to liquidate his assets; he is called to give as the Lord prospers him. The characteristic of Christian living is not communism, but charity.

The New Testament word for stewardship is the Greek *oikonomia,* from which we derive the English term "economy." It comes from a combination of two Greek roots, *oikos,* which means "house," and *nomos,* which means "law." Literally, "economy" means "house-rule." In antiquity the steward was not the owner of the house but its manager. He was responsible for the care and management of the house. Biblical economics recognizes God's ultimate ownership of the earth and man's duty to manage the earth responsibly.

The science of economics is not a neutral science divorced from ethical considerations. Economics involves questions of stewardship, the use of wealth, and private and public decisions of value, all of which impinge upon ethics. Each time we make a value judgment or render a decision to make use of material goods, we have made an ethical decision. That God is concerned with the material well-being of the world is axiomatic. Man has been called to be a steward of the earth.

The science of economics has become so complex in our day that it has obscured some of the primary principles found in the Scriptures. Though the Bible is not a textbook in economics, it does set forth basic principles that touch upon economic endeavor. As already mentioned, the Bible clearly sets forth the right of private property. But in addition to this right we also see a concern for equity, for industry, and for compassion. It is not by accident that virtually every major economic system in Western culture has appealed at one point or another to the Bible for its sanctions. Historic capitalism tends to emphasize the principles of private property and equity and industry, sometimes neglecting the responsibility for compassion. On the other hand, socialistic forms of economics have emphasized compassion, at times obscuring the rights of private property and undermining the importance of industry and equity. The socialist's ultimate goal is not equity but equality. That is, the socialist seeks a transfer society with the ideal of an egalitarian or equalized distribution of wealth. The goal is noble and virtuous; we would expect that in an idealized society, every member would have equal participation in the wealth of the society. But we live in a fallen world, where the only way we can have equality of economic welfare is to shut our eyes to the biblical principle of equity. We must penalize the producer and the industrious to take from them their goods and distribute them to those who have been less than responsible stewards. Such a principle does violence to the biblical notion of justice.

If we look at the most elementary principles of economics in their foundational form we see a causal nexus, a formula that must not be violated if we are to grapple with the economic issues of our day. The formula may be seen in the following diagram:

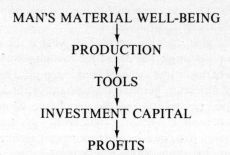

MAN'S MATERIAL WELL-BEING
↓
PRODUCTION
↓
TOOLS
↓
INVESTMENT CAPITAL
↓
PROFITS

We see that there is a causal relationship among these factors. The single most important ingredient for man's material well-being is production. If we are going to feed the hungry, clothe the naked, and give shelter to the homeless, we must be able to produce the goods necessary to meet these needs. Man's physical life is dependent upon production for human survival. Unless we produce food, we will starve; unless we manufacture clothes, we will be naked. Unless homes are built we will be shelterless. God does care about the human body as well as the human soul, and so production becomes a vital ethical concern for Christians.

If we follow our causal reasoning and ask what is the single most important necessary ingredient for production, we would answer, tools. Marx was astute in his understanding of the central significance of tools to man's increased capacity for production. The reason a peasant in a backward country cannot produce as much food as a farmer in the industrialized West is not that the body of the Western farmer is stronger but that the Western farmer has at his disposal labor-saving devices which increase production. The machine more than any other single factor has been responsible for the explosion of man's ability to produce.

The next question we raise is, what is the most important single ingredient for the acquisition of tools? Obviously that ingredient is capital. The primary difference between the peasant in the undeveloped nation and the Western farmer is at the level of tools. It is not that tools are not available in the world to be used by underprivileged persons but rather that those without money cannot purchase tools they need for increased production. Tools cost money to build, to buy, and to maintain.

Where does one get the money to purchase tools?

The needed capital is what we would call surplus capital. Surplus capital is a result of profits. Thus, profit is the single most important ingredient necessary for capital to be available to buy tools, to increase production, and to increase the material welfare of a nation. But the term "profit" has become virtually an obscenity in the vocabulary of modern man, particularly among Christians. What we often fail to take into account is that the profit motive is not restricted to large industrial corporations or the super-rich magnates and tycoons of industry. The profit motive is at the heart of all economic exchange. The goal or purpose of economic exchange is always and everywhere profit. This statement may appear on the surface to be outrageous, but let us take a moment to examine its implications.

When a business transaction takes place, when a customer buys a pair of shoes, who realizes a profit? Often the answer is that the shoe salesman or the owner of the shoe store makes the profit. But the shoemaker cannot make a profit unless first the customer considers it profitable for him to buy the shoes. The business transaction takes place when the customer values the shoes more than he values the money he must pay for them. Then trade takes place. The customer trades his money for the shoemaker's shoes. The shoemaker can in turn exchange that money for other goods that he values more than the money. Thus, in any business transaction the goal is mutual profit. Both sides must profit or the exchange will not take place, unless the exchange is made necessary by some form of external coercion. This principle is based on the fact that material values are subjective to the extent that not every person values everything to the same degree. The man who has a surplus of shoes but a lack of food will be eager to make a trade with the man who has a surplus of food but needs shoes. In the transaction one man values shoes more than meat, while the other values meat more than shoes, so a trade situation exists in which both persons profit according to the values they are seeking.

Profit is good in the sense that it is necessary for the whole community of mankind to survive in a relationship of mutual interdependency. No man is altogether self-sufficient. Each person is dependent to some degree on the gifts and talents of production of other people. The marketplace is where these gifts and talents are exchanged—a place of mutual profit, if the coercive dimension is absent. It is out of the surplus of profit that tools can be purchased, production increased, and the general wealth of the nation strengthened. Christians must remember this lest they become participants in schemes by which surplus capital is siphoned off and redistributed in a way that quenches the ability of a nation or a community to be productive.

The protection of private property is so vital to the biblical ethic that repeatedly we have prohibitions and sanctions against stealing. But stealing can happen in a multitude of ways, some of which are very subtle. The outright grabbing and carrying off of another person's property is an obvious form of stealing, but stealing can also be accomplished through fraud, by failing to live up to contracts, by using false weights and measures, or even by intentional debasing of currency within a society. All of these means receive the severe indictment of God.

One of the most subtle forms of theft is one that is perpetrated through the political system. When people use the power of the ballot box to vote for themselves largess or subsidies from the general coffers, it is a sophisticated form of stealing. For example, if three people live together in a town and one is more wealthy than the other two, the two persons of lesser wealth can conspire together to pass a law forcing the wealthier person to distribute his goods to them. Here the power of political force is used to strip the wealthy man of his wealth and distribute it to the other two, who have voted for themselves this particular distribution of wealth. Christians need to be sensitive about how they use the power of the ballot.

FIVE
THE ETHICS OF CAPITAL PUNISHMENT

The issue of capital punishment has been so volatile that it has set Christian against Christian, church against church, conservative against conservative, and liberal against liberal. The problem is complex, touching the deeper question of the value, dignity, and sanctity of human life. Any study of capital punishment must begin with an understanding of the primary function of government as originally ordained by God. Romans 13:1-7 is the classic text concerning God's ordination of government. This text is the most comprehensive and emphatic statement that the Scriptures give us regarding the notion that the power of government is rooted in the ordination of God. It is important to note that the Apostle is speaking here not of a theocratic state but of secular government. The text of Romans reads as follows:

Let every soul be subject unto the higher powers. For there is no power but of God: the powers that be are ordained of God. Whosoever therefore resists the power, resists the ordinance of God: and they that resist shall receive to themselves damnation. For rulers are not a terror to good works, but to the evil. Will you then not be afraid of the power? Do that which is good, and you shall have praise of the same: for he is the minister of God to you for good. But if you do that which is evil, be afraid; for he bears not the sword in vain: for he is the minister of God, a revenger to execute wrath upon him that does evil. Wherefore you must be subject, not only for wrath, but also for conscience sake. For this cause pay your taxes also: for they are God's ministers, attending continually upon this very thing. Render therefore to all their dues: taxes to whom taxes are due; custom to whom custom; fear to whom fear; honor to whom honor.

The "powers that be" are the powers that are understood to be ordained by God. We are not privileged to obey only those powers which we consider to be legitimate. It is a *de facto* matter, not a *de juro* matter. God certainly does not endorse everything civil magistrates do, but he does give them certain rights and requires our obedience to them. No government rules autonomously. All civil authorities must, and will, answer ultimately to God. We have the responsibility of obeying even corrupt governments except under certain conditions. Civil obedience is required repeatedly by the Word of God. The principle which governs our right and responsibility to disobey civil authority is this: we must obey those in authority over us unless they command us to do what God forbids or forbid us to do what God commands.

Biblically there are two basic rights that God has given to government: one, the right to levy taxes; two, the coercion of their subjects for the power of administering the state (the power of the sword).

Government was made necessary and legitimate because of the fall of man. The state was ordained to be God's deputy minister for the primary purpose of the restraint of evil. The first appearance of government in the Bible is found in the opening chapters of Genesis, when Adam and Eve are expelled from the garden and consigned to live east of Eden. The entrance to the garden is barred by the presence of an angel with a flaming sword. Here we see the appointment of a ministering agent, namely, the angel who is equipped by God with an instrument of restraint and is granted the power of coercion which is symbolized by the flaming sword.

The central duty of the government is to enforce the laws that are designed to restrain evil. It was St. Augustine who said, "Sin is the mother of servitude and is the first cause of man's subjection to man." Augustine argued that government is a necessary evil, in fact, an evil which is made necessary by the prior presence of evil in the human heart. It is because men are prone to violating each other that government is established to check the strong and ruthless who exploit and oppress the weak and the innocent. Government is necessary because men do not live to the glory of God, loving Him with all of their hearts and their neighbors as themselves. The only ultimate alternative to government is anarchy, in which each man lives for himself. Thus, government is instituted as an act of God's grace to protect the weak and the righteous from the wicked. The authority which the state possesses is not an intrinsic authority but that which is derived from the authority of God.

The issue of capital punishment emerges when we examine the right of the state to bear the sword. In the first instance the sword is seen as an instrument of coercion. I once had a conversation with a United States senator who said to me, "No government ever has the right to coerce its subjects to do anything." I was shocked by the senator's statement and replied, "Senator, you have just stated that no government has the right to govern." The power of coercion is the essence of government. Perhaps the simplest definition we can find for "government" is the word "force." In a very real sense government is force. If you take away the government's right to coerce, you take away the government's right to govern, leaving the government with the impotent authority of rule by suggestion. The power of the sword is the arm of the government which we call law enforcement, without which the law represents merely a list of suggestions. Nor did God give the sword to the civil magistrate as a means of intimidation for rattling only. In biblical categories the expression "power of the sword" is seen clearly as an idiomatic expression to indicate the power to kill.

At this point the issue of capital punishment comes to the fore. In the Old Testament we first read of the institution of capital punishment in the narrative of Creation. In the garden there was one restraint, one prohibition given to man. The clear-cut punishment for disobedience of this command was instant death. "The day that you shall eat of it, you shall surely die." It is important to note that when man sinned, God did not invoke the full measure of the punishment for disobedience. Indeed, capital punishment came upon the race but it was postponed in terms of its implementation. Originally all sin was regarded as a capital offense. Capital punishment was the divine judgment for any and all sin. However, God reserved the right to replace justice with mercy according to His own prerogatives. Because God has not executed that punishment consistently and immediately—except on rare occasions such as the case of Uzza, Nadab and Abihu, Ananias and Sapphira—the world tends to take God's mercy for granted and has come to the place where in some circles capital punishment is considered to be cruel and unusual punishment for any crime.

In the old covenant God reduced the number of capital offenses and limited the penalty to approximately thirty-five specific crimes. The New Testament exhibits an even more gracious dispensation, with a further reduction of capital offenses.

Before the institution of the law at Sinai we have an even more important statement, found in the covenant God made with Noah. Here we see a covenant which renews the ordinances of Creation, a renewal of God's rule for man as man. There is a certain sense in which the laws of this Creation covenant are of far broader import than even that legislation found in Israel or in the New Testament. Here God proposes legislation for man as man, not as man as Jew or man as Christian. Man *qua* man is the one who receives the stipulations of the covenant of Creation. It is therefore significant that capital punishment for murder is built into Creation and presumably is binding as long as Creation is intact. The renewal legislation is found in Genesis 9:6:

> Whoso sheds man's blood, by man shall his blood be shed: for in the image of God made he man.

This text is a command, not a future prediction. The sanction is clear. If a person murders another person, God requires that the murderer be put to death by human hands.

It is ironic that both sides of the dispute on capital punishment tend to base their arguments on the principle of the sanctity of life. The humanist argues that human life is so valuable that we are never justified in taking another person's life. From a biblical perspective the humanist view actually reflects a lower view of the sanctity of life than that found in Genesis 9:6. From the vantage point of the 20th century we tend to view the Old Testament society as severe and savage, forgetting that it already manifested an enormous reduction in capital offenses. These reductions in capital offenses did not come about because God changed his mind and saw that his former policies were too cruel and severe, but partially because the responsibility for the execution of justice in the New Testament moved out of the hands of the theocratic state and into the hands of the secular state.

The question as to how many crimes are considered "capital" in the New Testament is one that is open to lengthy debate. The only crime which we can be certain is a capital offense is first-degree murder. In the Decalogue of the Old Testament there is a clear prohibition against murder. But the broader legislation of Mount Sinai included within it several distinctions with respect to degrees of murder. The establishment of the cities of refuge, for example, dealt with the problem of involuntary manslaughter. The penalty for transgressing the prohibition in the Ten Commandments, "Thou shalt not kill," was capital punishment.

It is ironic that many have appealed to the Ten Commandments as a basis for repudiating capital punishment, taking the prohibition "Thou shalt not kill" as a universal mandate. This comes from a superficial reading of the Sinaitic legislation and a failure to observe that within the context of the Sinai covenant the penalty for violating that commandment was death. The holiness code of Israel clearly called for the death penalty in the case of the murder of another human being. The murderer must forfeit his own life. The reason given for the special sanctity of human life is the fact that man is created in the image of God. God is concerned with preserving the work of His creation, and at the top of His priorities is the preservation of the life of man. There is a sense in which the commission of murder is regarded by God as an indirect assault on Him. Just as an attack on an ambassador of a king is seen as an affront to the king, so the murderer is guilty of committing an assault against the very life of God, inasmuch as he has desecrated one made in His image. It is important to understand that power over life is not rescinded in the New Covenant but is mentioned again in Romans as a prerogative of the state. Thus, the Scriptures uniformly assert the propriety of capital punishment in the case of murder.

When we apply the principle of capital punishment to a given society or to a given culture, we must be careful lest we plunge into the matter without considering some of the other ramifications of the biblical sanctions. Though capital punishment was imposed in the Old Testament, it was circumscribed by other principles that were very important to the entire justice process. In the Old Testament, justice was truly blind under the law. The rich were to be given no special privileges before the bar of justice. That ideal exists in our own society, but at a practical level there are too many circumstances in which Lady Justice peeks or removes her blindfold altogether to take note of the rich and the powerful who are her suitors. Under the Old Covenant no one could be convicted of a capital offense on the basis of circumstantial evidence. Two or three eye witnesses were required and their testimony had to agree. If the witnesses who testified in a capital trial were found guilty of perjury, the penalty for bearing such false witness was itself death. There is no question that we need reforms to protect inequities of the application of capital punishment in our modern culture, but when we raise objection to capital punishment in principle, we are objecting to a sanction God Himself ordained.

SIX
THE ETHICS OF WAR

The issue of a Christian's involvement in war is an extension of the more primary question of capital punishment. In a certain sense war is capital punishment on a grand scale. It involves the civil magistrates' widespread use of the power of the sword. Basically there have been three foundational positions which have been taken regarding war in past Christian history:

1. Activism
2. Pacifism
3. Selectivism

Activism is a simplistic approach to war which views all wars as being permissable. It reflects the position that the subjects of the state are to give absolute obedience to the civil magistrate regardless of the situation. It reflects the simple cliché "My country, right or wrong." This is basically an uncritical approach which has little to do with the biblical ethic.

Pacifism, on the other hand, says that all wars are wrong and all people's involvement in war is wrong. The pacifist view would restrict Christians from participating in any kind of war.

The third variety is called selectivism, which maintains that involvement in some wars may be justifiable. It is within the context of selectivism that the basis for the just war theory has emerged in Christian history.

A sophisticated argument by pacifists who are Christians is based on the ethical mandates Christ gave His people, whereby He prohibited the Christian from the use of retaliatory violence and uttered a clear prohibition against building His kingdom with the sword. The pacifist transfers these prohibitions from the sphere of the church to the sphere of government. Here not only is the private citizen or the ecclesiastical authority forbidden the use of the sword but the state is prohibited as well. Some divide the question by admitting that the state has the power of the sword, but Christians are not to participate in the state's function. The question that is raised immediately is, "On what grounds would a Christian refuse to obey a civil magistrate who calls the Christian to do something that is within the scope of righteousness?" If God commands the state to bear the sword and the state conscripts the Christian to help him with that task, on what moral grounds could the Christian possibly refuse to comply?

The Swiss theologian Emil Brunner has remarked, "To deny on ethical grounds the elementary right of the state to defend itself by war simply means to deny the existence of the state itself. Pacifism of the absolutist variety is practical anarchy." Helmut Thielicke has added his judgment that pacifism is a moral cop-out. He draws a parallel between pacifism and a situation where the Christian is a witness to murder and stands by and allows it to happen without interference. Thielicke argues that it is not only our responsibility to minister to a man who has been mutilated by robbers, such as the man going down to Jericho, but we are to love our neighbor by preventing the crime as well.

Selectivism proceeds from the fundamental premise that all wars are wrong but that not everyone's involvement in a war is wrong. The particular circumstances and situations must be evaluated on each occasion to discern which side, if either, has a righteous cause to defend. The victim of a clear-cut act of aggression would have the right of self-defense, according to the selective view.

SEVEN
THE ETHICS
OF ABORTION

Abortion is a monumental issue which excites a great amount of emotional action. Divisions in the state and in the church are multiplying, with major denominational church bodies coming down on both sides of the issue. The fires of controversy show no signs of abating, but rather of intensifying.

In dealing with this issue, three major questions must be answered:

1. What is abortion?
2. Is abortion right or is it wrong? Or is it possibly without moral bearing?
3. Does the church have the right to advocate civil legislation on this question? Some church bodies have advocated a "middle way" under the rubric of "pro-choice," arguing that this

should be a matter of conscience, not of civil legislation, and that it is wrong for the state to prohibit abortion.

BIBLICAL BASIS FOR DISCUSSION

No teaching in the Old Testament or New Testament explicitly condemns or condones abortion. Exegetically, the debate has been waged on implicit grounds. The Old Testament passage which has received the sharpest attention is Exodus 21: 22-25.

If men strive, and hurt a woman with child, so that her fruit depart from her, and yet no mischief follow: He shall be surely punished, according as the woman's husband will lay upon him; and he shall pay as the judges determine. And if any mischief follow, then thou shalt give life for life, eye for eye, tooth for tooth, hand for hand, foot for foot . . . .

There is a built-in ambiguity with this text, giving rise to differing interpretations of its precise meaning and application. The theological house is divided between "maximum" and "minimum" positions. The problem centers in the words "no mischief follow." To what "mischief" does the verse refer? This problem is linked to another, namely the question of what is meant by the "fruit departing" from the pregnant woman. Is the text referring to an incident in which the woman, being jostled by fighting men, is induced to a premature childbirth in which the anguish and inconvenience of premature delivery is recompensed by the law even though the premature child lives and thrives? Or is the text speaking of a case where the induced premature birth yields a stillborn fetus and further considerations come into play only if the mother suffers additional complications, even death?

The Old Testament scholar Keil adopts the maximum view, arguing that the "no mischief follow" clause refers to both mother and child. The summary is that if the premature baby survives, recompense is limited to damages paid for the inconvenience and mental anguish provoked as claimed by the husband and awarded by the judge. But if the child is harmed or dies, the full measure of the *lex talonis* (eye for eye) is to apply. In this reading the unborn fetus is so highly valued by Scripture that the life-for-life principle is applied and the unintentional causing of abortion "in the midst of another felonious act" warrants the death penalty. If this interpretation is correct, we would have decisive evidence that Scripture considers the unborn fetus as "life" in the fullest legal sense.

The minimal view of the text argues that the "no mischief follow" clause refers exclusively to the mother. In this schema the net result would be that the aborted or premature birth of the fetus would not invoke the *lex talonis* or legally be considered murder or loss of life. Only if further complications affect the mother does the "eye for eye, life for life" equation apply. The inference then would be that Scripture does not regard the fetus as "life." The fetus is protected by the law, however, and its *value* may be established via law suit. Some push it further by arguing that though legal indemnities *may* be imposed, they are initiated by the claims of the husband. The unspoken presumption is that the "value" of the fetus is determined to some degree by the subjective values attached by the parents. In this "case" the Scriptures deal with an abortion or miscarriage imposed from without, apart from the design of the parents, who presumably desire the pregnancy to reach its full term. The passage is then made of no consequence to the question of an intentional abortion performed according to the will and design of the parents. The minimal view thus protects the parents and not the fetus.

The difference between these interpretations covers the gamut of the contemporary debate. Though I am persuaded of the maximal interpretation, I must admit the problematic and ambiguous character of the text.

In the New Testament the word "abortion" is used only in a figurative sense. One passage which is often cited to support an anti-abortion stance is Luke 1:39-42, when Mary visited Elizabeth and the child "leaped in her womb." Other references which refer to persons being conceived in sin and known by God in the womb are also referred to. The question exegetically is whether or not these allusions are to be taken as religious hyperbole or poetry. However, the message of these passages clearly indicates that God is involved with man's history prior to his birth.

The question of when life begins has been pivotal to the discussion. Agreement is difficult because no consensus has emerged. Different points on the conception-birth continuum have been proferred, with the added problem of variant medical definitions of "life" itself.

There are some who maintain that the moment of birth is when a fetus becomes a person. There are good reasons for this argument. This is a rather clear line of demarcation, indicating a new status, a new moment of independent existence with *individuation* beginning with the snipping of the umbilical cord.

Another view points to the moment of "quickening"; another to the time when the circulatory system is fully developed. Others say that the principle of life in the Old Testament is the "breath" of life in man. Therefore, life would be present when the lungs develop and the fetus could breathe on its own.

The moment of conception has been seen by many groups to be the beginning of life, since all the potentiality of personhood is then present. David and others speak of their conception as part of their personal history.

What the fetus is (what we conceive it to be) will determine what value we assign it. There are those who say that the embryo (the term usually used to refer to the product of conception during its first twelve weeks) is nothing more than a blob of protoplasm. Others argue that it is merely a highly specialized form of parasite. It has been compared to a cancer, a tissue growth foreign to the mother, which the body seeks to reject. If the mother fails to reject it, it would be fatal to her. Certainly these are emotive terms which greatly cloud the issue and represent an irresponsible approach to the question.

To refer to an embryo as a blob of protoplasm is to be guilty of a severe form of reductionism. The "parasite" term is equally inaccurate, as parasites have an independent life cycle which includes reproduction. As for the analogy to cancer, a cancer left to natural development destroys life. An embryo left to natural development produces life—a difference which may hardly be ignored.

The crucial concern here is that we can say with certainty that at any stage of development the fetus is a potential life, a potential human being, with a high level of probability of becoming a human being, if left to nature. With this in mind, let us look at the essence of the debate: What is the relationship of abortion to the biblical prohibition against murder? Does the Bible have anything to say about the *destruction of a potential life?*

We remember that in the Old Testament there are five distinctions made in the broader application of the Decalogue's prohibition of killing, including distinctions for manslaughter and involuntary murder. In the New Testament, however, we have an authoritative application and interpretation of this prohibition.

The prohibition "Thou shalt not kill" is not a universal prohibition against all taking of human life, but it is wider in its scope than simple first-degree murder. Jesus includes in his understanding of this mandate a prohibition against hatred. Hatred is understood as murder of the heart. In effect Jesus says that the law implicitly prohibits *potential murder* (and *potential adultery*). Left to its own, hatred results in murder; lust, in adultery. He says that the law prohibits the *potential destruction of life.* This is not the same as prohibiting the *actual destruction of potential life.* But these two are very close to being the same, similar enough to raise serious questions about abortion. In terms of the sanctity of life, potentiality is clearly an issue with Jesus.

If we are seriously considering the spirit of the law, we must pay attention to the implications (implicit understanding) of a particular commandment. The converse of a prohibition must be affirmed: what the law implicitly affirms is a part of the complex of what the prohibition explicitly negates. Wanton destruction of life is prohibited. This implies an implicit command to promote the sanctity and safeguarding of life. The sanctity of life is the supreme basis for the prohibition of murder. The question is, does the sanctity of life include concern for potential life? There is no way we can prove decisively that it does. But in light of the overwhelming concern in the Scriptures for the safeguarding and preservation of life, the burden of proof must be on those who wish to destroy potential life.

Perhaps the strongest case for the support of liberal abortion laws is the right of the mother. Some groups have countered this with the issue of the right of the unborn. But the root of the matter goes deeper. The issue biblically is between the concept of the woman's right and the woman's responsibility. Does the woman have the right to disrupt natural law? Is she responsible for the natural consequences of her voluntary acts? Relative to this debate is the fact that we do not have absolute rights over our own bodies within the sphere of Creation. Self-mutilation is forbidden within the Old Testament. If mutilation before conception is wrong, what about mutilation after conception?

Another argument used to support legalized abortion is the utilitarian argument, which opts for the lesser of two evils. The argument is that under the present restrictions, the only abortions that are available (apart from therapeutic abortions) are those obtained illegally, which are often hazardous. To protect people from their own foolish acts, wisdom would dictate legalizing abortion. This argument is irrelevant to the question of whether or not abortion is right. Committing a felony is also a dangerous business, but the danger is no justification for the legalization of bank robbery.

The issue of therapeutic abortions must be dealt with separately. Generally they are used in two situations: where there is clear and present danger to the life and physical health of the mother, and where there is concern for the psychological well-being of the mother, especially in the case where the woman has been victimized by a rapist. In the first instance, there are two basic points. Some argue that in the case of the danger to the life of the mother, it is better to destroy the fetus to save the mother. The actual life is more valuable than the potential life. Others say the fetus should be saved, basing this on the matter of certainty vs. probability. Suppose that the death of the mother is 99 percent probable if the child is left to be born. If there is an abortion, that means 100 percent certainty of death for the fetus. If there is one chance in 100 for both to survive, this group holds that the chance should be taken.

The final question is that of church and state. Many Christians have taken the position that it is not the church's business what the state legislates, since the church is not to legislate morality. However, the state *does* have the responsibility of legislating morality. Traffic laws deal with the moral issue of how one drives one's car. Justice is a moral issue; laws are an attempt to promote justice. The essence of legislation is morality. The church has the responsibility to speak to the legislature. The state's primary function is the preservation of society and the preservation of life. When the state is involved in legislation that does not respect and promote the sanctity of life, the church must speak out. While we recognize the separation of power between church and state, we cannot recognize the autonomy of the state before God. The state is also a servant of God. If there is any legislation on which the church has the responsibility to speak, it is on this one, since the heart of the issue is the sanctity of life.

The debate within the church tends to focus on the *tertium quid,* the third option, known as the "Right to Choice" position, one which has steadily grown in popularity.

Evidence is emerging that the strategy of pro-abortionists, led by Planned Parenthood, has been the oldest strategy of all: "divide and conquer." Main-line Protestant bodies have been solicited to aid the cause of pro-abortion on the grounds that human rights are being violated by the oppressive tyranny of a Roman Catholic monolith. Eager to stand against tyranny and for human rights, countless Protestant clergy and denominations have endorsed the middle ground between the combatants of pro-life and pro-abortion. The *via media,* or moderate middle, has been defined as the pro-choice position.

Two vital questions must be faced by those wrestling with the premier moral issue of our day. The first question is, "What is the practical difference between pro-abortion and pro-choice?" In terms of legislation a vote for pro-choice is a vote for pro-abortion, which the pro-abortionists understand clearly. No one knows the exact figures, but it is obvious from the polls that a large group of voters, if not a plurality of them, favor the middle ground. Certainly it is this middle position that has swung the balance of legislative power and the weight of public opinion to the side of the pro-abortionists. We hear it said repeatedly, "I would not choose to have an abortion, but I think every woman has a right to make that choice for herself."

In this statement the focus is upon the concept of a human "right." The mother is said to have the right over her own body to bear a child or to dispose of the fetus. (The central issue is not about victims of rape or mothers endangered by childbirth; the issue before us is abortion-on-demand-for-convenience.) This presses the second question: "What constitutes a moral right and from whence come moral rights?"

As Christians we recognize, I hope, that there is a profound difference between a moral right and a legal right. Ideally legal rights reflect moral rights, but such is not always the case. How does one establish the moral right to choose abortion? From the law of nature? From the law of God? Hardly. Natural law abhors abortion and divine law implicitly condemns it.

The real basis of the right to choose abortion is based on want. The unspoken assumption of the right-to-choice position is the assumption that I am free to choose whatever I want—an assumption repugnant to both God and nature. I never have the moral right to do evil. I may have the civil and legal right to sin but never the moral right. The only moral rights I have are to righteousness.

Is not the issue more complex? Does it not hang together with the broader issue of the extent of government intrusion into our private lives? Surely it does. I know few stronger advocates of limited government than myself. I abhor the proliferating tendrils of government pressing into our lives. But the primary purpose of government, biblically, is to exercise restraint on mankind in order to promote, preserve, and protect the sanctity of life. This is the very *raison d'être* of human government.

If abortion-on-demand is evil, no one has the moral right to choose it. If it is an offense against life, the government must not permit it. The day is being captured by the moderate middle who have not faced the ethical implications of this position. This is the moral cop-out of our day—the shame of our churches and her leaders. It is time to get off the fence. Pro-choice is pro-abortion. Be clear about that and abandon the muddled middle.

EIGHT
ETHICS AND
THE CONSCIENCE

The function of the conscience in ethical decision-making tends to complicate matters for us. The commandments of God are eternal, but in order to obey them we must first appropriate them internally. The "organ" of such internalization has been classically called the conscience. Some describe this nebulous inner voice as the voice of God within. The conscience is a mysterious part of man's inner being. Within the conscience, in a secret hidden recess, lies the personality, so hidden that at times it functions without our being immediately aware of it. When Freud brought hypnosis into the palace of respectable scientific inquiry, men began to explore the subconscious and examine those intimate caverns of the personality. Encountering the conscience can be an awesome experience. The uncovering of the inner voice can be, as one psychiatrist notes, like "looking into hell itself."

Yet we tend to think of conscience as a heavenly thing, a point of contact with God, rather than a hellish organ. We think of the cartoon character faced with an ethical decision while an angel is perched on one shoulder and a devil on the other, playing tug-of-war with the poor man's head. The conscience can be a voice from heaven or hell; it can lie as well as press us to truth. It is a voice with two sides to its mouth, having the capacity either to *accuse* or to *excuse*.

Walt Disney made popular the jingle, "Let your conscience be your guide." This is at best Jiminy Cricket theology. For the Christian the conscience is not the highest court of appeals for right conduct. The conscience is important, but not normative. It is capable of distortion and misguidance. It is mentioned some thirty-one times in the New Testament with abundant indication of its capacity for change. The conscience can be seared and eroded, being desensitized by repeated sin. Jeremiah described Israel as having the "forehead of the harlot." From repeated transgressions Israel had, like the prostitute, lost her capacity to blush. With the stiffened neck and the hardened heart came also the calloused conscience. The sociopath can murder without remorse, being immune to the normal pangs of conscience.

Though the conscience is not the highest tribunal of ethics, it is perilous to act against it. We remember Luther at the Diet of Worms, trembling in agony at the enormous moral pressure he was facing. When asked to recant, he included these words in his reply: "My conscience is held captive by the Word of God. To act against conscience is neither right nor safe."

Luther's graphic use of the word "captive" illustrates the visceral power the compulsion of conscience can exercise on a person. Once a person is gripped by the voice of conscience, a power is harnessed by which acts of heroic courage may issue forth. A conscience captured by the Word of God is both noble and powerful.

Was Luther correct in saying, "To act against conscience is neither right nor safe"? Here we must tread carefully lest we slice our toes on the ethical razor's edge. If the conscience can be misinformed or distorted, why should we not act against it? Should we follow our consciences into sin? Here we have a dilemma of the double jeopardy sort. If we follow our consciences into sin, we are still guilty of sin inasmuch as we are required to have our consciences rightly informed by the Word of God. However, if we act against our consciences, we are also guilty of sin. The sin may not be located in what we do but rather in the fact that we committed an act we believed to be evil. Here the biblical principle that whatever is not of faith is sin comes into play. For example, if a person is taught and comes to believe that wearing lipstick is a sin and then wears lipstick, that person is sinning. The sin resides not in the lipstick but in the *intent* to act against what one believes to be the command of God.

The dilemma of double jeopardy demands that we diligently strive to bring our consciences into harmony with the mind of Christ lest a carnal conscience lead us into disobedience. We require a redeemed conscience, a conscience of the spirit rather than the flesh.

The manipulation of conscience can be a destructive force within the Christian community. Legalists are often masters of guilt manipulation while antinomians master the art of quiet denial. The conscience is a delicate instrument which must be respected. One who seeks to influence the consciences of others carries a heavy responsibility to maintain the integrity of the other person's own personality as crafted by God. When we impose false guilt on others we paralyze our neighbors, binding them in chains where God has left them free. When we urge false innocence we contribute to their delinquency, exposing them to the judgment of God.

CONCLUSION

The Christian life is a life lived by principles, principles drawn from the character of God via sacred Scripture. The knowledge provided by ethics supplies weapons for only half the moral struggles we face. We fight a war on two fronts, meeting two perplexing difficulties. Our first problem is to discern the good. Our second problem is to muster the moral courage to do the good. It is entirely possible that we know what is right, yet lack the moral strength to do it. The study of ethics offers help in the battle on both fronts. By mastering the biblical principles of righteousness we can begin to escape the gray area of confusion. With greater assurance of what God requires we are less vulnerable to the seduction of moral compromise. A clarity of understanding strengthens the will as it enlightens the mind. To be sure, the clear understanding of the right does not guarantee the actual performance of it. For that we require grace upon grace. Yet the understanding assists and undergirds the will by strengthening the voice of a godly conscience. Our goal is to do the will of God and "this," says the Scripture, "is the will of God for you, even your sanctification."